That
Someone
The Script

Chiquita Hayes, M.D.

Order this book online at www.trafford.com
or email orders@trafford.com

Most Trafford titles are also available at major online book retailers.

Printed in the United States of America.

ISBN: 978-1-4669-6534-8 (sc)
ISBN: 978-1-4669-6535-5 (e)

Library of Congress Control Number: 2012920113

Trafford rev. 01/16/2013

 www.trafford.com

North America & international
toll-free: 1 888 232 4444 (USA & Canada)
phone: 250 383 6864 ♦ fax: 812 355 4082

IN LOVE,

This work is dedicated to:

THE FATHER

THE SON

and

THE HOLY SPIRIT.

PLEASE NOTE:

The text of "That Someone" is an original work.

The order of the First and Second Cups in "The Bread and the Wine" section is adapted from:

> *Passover Haggadah*
> KF Holdings, Inc. 2003. pp. 6-8; 26-28

If you are hosting "That Someone",

Please read the Host's Guidelines

in the Appendix before you begin.

Thank you.

TESTIMONIES

I have enjoyed the phenomenon of the Seder that Chiquita Hayes has perfected in her labor of love that we have experienced over the years. It has been a blessing to me as a believer. I have learned to appreciate more the significance of our Jewish heritage.

Janice Coleman
Janice Coleman Corporation

I grew up with the Seder. Each year it has gotten better.
It's fun, interactive, and perfect for all ages! It is a great way to get together with family and celebrate the Resurrection of our Lord.

Stephanie Coleman
(age 19)

I have been at the Seder every year for nearly my whole life.
I have fun reading with the other kids and finding the hidden matzo.
I also have learned a lot about covenants.

Daniel Coleman
(age 12)

My family and I experienced an exciting time together with other families as we were partakers of our first Seder at the Hayes'. It was a powerful and enlightening event that caused us to appreciate our salvation even more. Truly we are all one new man in Christ!

We look forward to the next one. We, as a family, will never be the same. Thank you for making it a clear reality in our hearts and minds.

Dr. Rosa Drummond
Redeemed Worship Center Church

I remember approaching the first Seder celebration several years ago with much anticipation. I was not disappointed. I have watched as, over the years, new insights, revelations, and adjustments were woven into the delicate fabric of this teaching. Each year this celebration has been new and affirming of the "blood covenant".

The truths revealed in the understanding of the blood covenant have truly revolutionized my personal governing theology. After experiencing the Seder I have realized a new understanding of the New Covenant and the celebration of the Communion through the perspective of the blood covenant. The elements of the blood covenant-making process: the exchanges, the blessings (and the potential curses), covenant-ratifying meal, all create a powerful message of the importance of understanding this celebration on a higher and deeper personal and corporate level. We truly have access to all the resources of heaven, not just salvation, because God has cut covenant with us through His Son.

The celebration of the Communion is an invitation to a grand meal with God. The "bread of the Presence" and the drink that symbolizes His powerful, life-giving blood, create an atmosphere of cleansing and deep heart change that then enables us to walk in the power of His love and grace. When we incorporate these life-enriching truths into our corporate and personal Communion, His powerful presence manifests itself in greater measure than that which we typically experience.

May you be blessed in the same way that I have been these many years by these truths.

Rev. Jim White

PREFACE

I am grateful to God for showing me a special dimension of His glory as revealed in the true meaning of the Passover Seder. I experienced a Seder as a high school student through a counselor's invitation. Therefore, many years later when I heard about the Christian version being hosted by Phil and Chiquita Hayes, I was excited and wanted to be a part of it. The revelation that I received through that Holy Sacred Seder solidified and significantly enhanced my perception of God, His blood covenant and His willingness to keep that covenant.

Each year, my family and I have attended this anointed time of fellowshipping with Father, The Lord Jesus, and Holy Spirit.

Each year we have seen strategic breakthroughs as a result of attending and participating in this experience. Each year the revelation given to us by Holy Spirit through Dr. Chiquita Hayes has grown deeper and more generous, producing life-changing *and* life-saving illumination.

This year's Seder was the greatest yet, filled with an inherent momentum of deeper growth within the hearts of those who participate in this experience. This revelation is long overdue, and the time is certainly now for the Body of Christ to receive this word from the Lord.

Thank you to the Hayes family for being so faithful to host this most glorious event year after year.

Thank you, Dr. Chiquita Hayes, for giving yourself sacrificially to birth this work so that the generations of believers to come might, once and for all, experience Holy Communion Seder the way Jesus *always* intended for it to be experienced.

I believe that this work will be THE VEHICLE to bring to pass the words of Jesus:

> "But I say unto you, I will not drink of this fruit of the vine from now on until that day when I drink it new **with you** in My Father's kingdom." (Matthew 26:29)

Thanks be unto God for this most unspeakable GIFT!

Pastor Derek F. Wilson
Body Life Support Ministries, Inc.

ACKNOWLEDGMENTS

Many thanks to everyone who participated, encouraged and prayed for this work over the years.

Thanks and gratitude to those who have been a source of support and strength year after year:

> the Colemans, the Drummonds, the Kelly Johnson family,
> the Marshalls, Jean Martinas, the Rich family (in loving memory of "Mr. Bob"),
> the Roanes, the Roberts (in loving memory of Sheila),
> the Serrano's, the Wilsons (in loving memory of "Mom" Evelyn),
> the Witherspoons.

Many thanks to Pastor Derek Wilson, Rev. William Roane, and Kelly Johnson, and all of Body Life Support Ministries, for their generous and enthusiastic support.

My family thanks our pastors, Apostle Abraham and Dr. Eve Fenton, Rev. Aubrey Fenton, and all of the Apostolic Council of Abundant Life Fellowship, for their kindness and excellent leadership.

We also thank Pastor Richard Minus for speaking into our lives through the years.

My loving thanks to the Abundant Life Intercessory Prayer Group, the Abundant Life Food Bank, and to Cheryl Marshall, my faithful prayer partner.

Much love to my family for their hard work, encouragement, prayers and commitment to "That Someone":

My husband: Dr. Phillip Hayes, Sr.
My daughters: Christina, Kelly, and Jennifer
My son and daughter-in-law: Phillip and Elizabeth

Love you all!

Chiquita Hayes

CONTENTS

". . . and in thee and in thy seed shall all the families of the earth be blessed."

Genesis 28:14 (KJV)

"Now to Abraham and his seed were the promises made. He saith not, And to seeds, as of many; but as of one, AND TO THY SEED, which is Christ."

Galatians 3:16 (KJV)

Our Prayer:

Father, in the name of Jesus, may this celebration bring us all into a new experience of Your love and friendship. May we find a deeper appreciation of the greatness of Your plan of salvation, the power of Your blood covenant, the love with which You love us, and the fellowship of Your presence.

May our lives be forever changed into the image of Jesus Christ, and may we reveal that image to those around us. We do all these things in Your honor and for Your glory.

Amen.

In His love,

Chiquita Hayes and family and friends

Among the holy angels of God, a saying once circulated. No one was quite sure of its origin. Some said one of the ancient scribe angels had copied it from the wise conversations between The Father, The Son, and The Holy Spirit. Others suggested that an esteemed teacher in the angelic academies stated the phrase in a moment of enlightenment that teachers sometimes have. Most feel that a humble lowly angel, while writing in his daily journal, realized this truth.

All great heavenly stories open with those wonderful words:
In the beginning . . .

On the other hand, whimsical human stories often say:
Once upon a time . . .

And yet, a story exists from the time when there was no time:
This story is truly to be believed!

THE PEOPLE AND THE BLOOD COVENANT

Introduction

Host: The angels realized what the Heavenly Father already knew: the people of Earth needed help.

Guest: This help could only flow from The Father, The Son, and The Holy Spirit.

Guest: This help could only come from Their hearts of mercy and love.

Guest: This love, which brought life and light to all of Heaven's universe, brought great joy and comfort to the angelic hosts.

Host: A question, however, arose among angelic circles in quiet conversations: How had the humans, Adam and Eve, misunderstood the love of God?

Guest: Some said that maybe humans were too smart for their own good.

Guest: Others were convinced that the one who had tried to start trouble in Heaven, took his troublemaking skills to Earth.

Guest: In any case, those who were made in God's image and likeness ignored a simple truth: they were already like God, with the power to love, to forgive, to subdue, to change.

Guest: Instead, they allowed the enemy of God to poison their lives through sin and disobedience.

Guest: "I was afraid" became the force that drove humanity and blotted out the light of Heaven.

Guest: Without that light the true path back to Heaven became a mystery, hidden in the folds of a universe that responded to faith on earth and words from Heaven.

Guest: Without that light the darkness grew.

Guest: Only two things now stood between the encroaching darkness and fallen humanity . . .

Guest: . . . a great promise from their rich and merciful God . . .

Guest: . . . and the blood of an innocent Lamb . . .

Host: When humanity fell, The Lord God gave Adam and Eve a promise . . . a glimpse of the light that leads to a glorious rescue . . .

Guest: . . . a Someone Who would bring down the highly exalted status of the enemy . . .

Guest: . . . Someone Who would bring blessings to every family on the earth . . .

Guest: But how, the angels wondered, would the Lord God bring blessings back into the lives of people ensnared in the adversary's grasp?

Host: Then the Lord God did a strange thing! He covered Adam and Eve in the skins of sacrificial animals who had given their innocent blood.

Guest: And an understanding passed between the Lord God and His human creation . . .

Guest: . . . that until "That Someone" came, the lives of bulls, goats, and lambs would be given to cover fallen humanity's emptiness.

Guest: The mercy of Heaven was hidden in the blood of these sacrificial animals.

Host: When these offerings were given to Him in holiness, the Lord God would forgive and have compassion on His creation.

Guest: And so, an awareness arose in angelic circles that, while The Lord God was willing for the fallen angels to face certain doom, He was *unwilling* to have His human creation endure the same destruction.

Guest: A moment came, therefore, when Heaven sent a lifeline to humanity through a special man named Abraham.

Guest: An awareness then arose in Abraham's descendants that this lifeline was the blood covenant agreement that sprang from the love and mercy of God.

Guest: This agreement was based on eternal promises made in Heaven before creation began.

Host: An eternal promise of rescue, given by The Son, that if a human body were prepared for Him, He would go to earth and redeem captive humanity.

Guest: An eternal promise of fatherhood, made by the Lord God, that He would be His Father and not abandon Him.

Guest: An eternal promise of revelation, made by the Holy Spirit, that He would show The Son the path back to Heaven.

Guest: These promises, sealed in love and covered in glory, became the anchor of hope in which the blood covenant was grounded.

Host: And soon the angels realized that the Father's heart held a special place for that puzzling creation called "people."

Entering the Blood Covenant

Host: The angelic puzzlement over human life was not restricted just to them. Most people on earth were puzzled as well. "Should I do this or that? Go here or there? Trust this one or that one? Maybe neither? Maybe both?"

Guest: Life was bewildering.

Guest: Most people found that they needed something to hold onto, a guarantee.

Guest: Many put their trust in the blood covenant agreement.

Guest: So let's look at some ways in which the blood covenant solidified the faith of those involved.

Host: Let's be sure to remember that life is different today than it was in ancient societies. We do not need to shed blood to enter into agreements or to get the Lord's attention. Now we have written and verbal contracts. Now we have the written Word of God, which speaks to us of the blood covenant that was "cut" between The Father, The Son and The Holy Spirit; that transfuses all of the covenants given by God to His people: that brought Jesus to earth to be the final sacrifice for sin forever!

No longer does the blood of animals have to be poured on an altar.

No longer does human blood (which God **never** asked for nor required) have to be shed.

The blood of Jesus Christ settles all issues and guarantees all of Heaven's promises.

However, we can gain insight into the heart of God as we see how two friends in ancient times would enter the blood covenant.

Let's follow this scenario. May our two volunteers come forward?

The story begins with two friends, Adams and Bailey, who each have a dream.

Adams is a painter and carpenter who crafts furniture, but has no means of selling or distributing the products.

But Adams does have a valuable asset: a friend.

Bailey has just inherited a stall at the local open-air market, but has no idea what to do with it.

Bailey also has a valuable asset: a friend.

Through this friendship a business is born that is guaranteed by the blood covenant.

So, how does this work?

The blood covenant between friends became an extension of the lifeline that Heaven had given to Earth.

It became a statement of "strong friendship," of "blood (covenant blood) being thicker than water."

The joy and responsibility of being "a friend who sticks closer than a brother" became a monumental decision, for it said, "I'm giving up my old life to share a new one with you."

Guest: What did these two friends end up doing?

Host: Let's find out!

> ADAMS: Hey, Bailey! Looks like you've got a nice place here.
>
> BAILEY: Thanks. I just inherited it from my folks. They just bought some tents out by the Red Sea. You know, hit the water, do some fishing, that kind of thing.
>
> ADAMS: Sounds great! Do they ever send you some fish, so you can make a few bucks in the fish market?
>
> BAILEY: Are you kidding? I've been closed for the past three weeks trying to get the smell of stinky fish out of here! They may be fresh

when they catch them, but by the time they get here—hold your nose!

ADAMS: So the fish business was a bust.

BAILEY: Completely! In fact, I'm thinking of closing altogether and moving to the shore.

ADAMS: OK that's great . . . Hey, wait . . . before you do that . . . ever thought of opening a furniture store?

Host: So, the first thing our friends do is to decide that this is a good business deal and one that a "strong friendship" can support.

Once the decision is made, they give themselves a few days to *really* think about it.

During that time, they eat, they sleep, they work, they talk.

They decide:

BAILEY: It's a great idea!

ADAMS: Let's do it!

BAILEY: I'll get that fish smell out of here before we open.

ADAMS: Thanks, pal.

Host: Now our two friends go through a series of exchanges.

They exchange outer coats:

> BAILEY: Here, you can have my navy blue blazer.

> ADAMS: Cool. You can have my fleece jacket.

> By doing this they are saying, "my position in society is yours."

Guest: The friends would then exchange or join names.

Guest: "Bailey's Fish Market" would now become: "Bailey's and Adams' Furniture Spot."

Host: Another step is to exchange something that shows their strength in life.

> BAILEY: Here's the key to the stall, I mean the spot. Move your furniture in anytime.

> ADAMS: Here's my tool belt. Any piece you see that needs fixing, it's all yours!

Guest: By doing this, they establish trust, and say to each other that they share their strengths and overcome each other's weaknesses.

Guest: A point comes, however, when the friends must go beyond symbolic gestures and step into the eternity of the blood covenant.

Host: Yes, the moment came for the blood of a sacrificial animal to be shed and poured out.

> The animal was cut down the mid-line along the backbone, and the halves were laid open.

This moment became a sacred one, for The Lord God had said, "the life of the flesh is in the blood."

Guest: As the blood soaked into the soil, the two covenant friends walk down the middle or walk in a figure eight.

Guest: This symbolizes the eternal nature of their covenant agreement.

Guest: As they walk, they rehearse the blessings that will come and the penalties that await if the covenant is broken.

Host: And so some of the blessings might go like this:

BAILEY: May our business expand overseas!

ADAMS: May our profits last for a thousand generations!

BAILEY: May we advertise on TV and have great infomercials!

ADAMS: May celebrities, royalty, and professional athletes buy our furniture!

Host: But there are potential consequences for breaking this agreement, such as:

BAILEY: If you sue me, may you lose and have to pay me a million dollars!

ADAMS: If you break this covenant, may someone steal your Ferrari!

Host: Yes, the consequences were real. However, the true motivation behind the blood covenant is love, and the realization that life is better if we are joined together than if we are separated.

          The walking through the blood became a step of faith for a "life exchange."

          In effect this said:

          "Like this animal, my individual life has died, and now I walk in the life of its blood, in new life with you."

Guest: The shedding of the animal's blood sealed the covenant agreement, making it a legal transaction in Heaven and on earth.

Guest: The sealing of this covenant agreement says that our two friends here share a common destiny and goal: the success of their business.

Guest: Each one has access to the strength, wisdom and resources of the other, if necessary.

Guest: We say, "if necessary", because the blood covenant of The Lord God was designed to be a gateway of blessing, not an opportunity for greed and abuse.

Host: The covenant bond means that if one succeeds, the other succeeds. If one has wealth and influence, so does the other. Every debt is absorbed, every difficulty faced together.

          A covenant meal was eaten, and a memorial tree or heap of stones was given as a witness to this new life.

ADAMS: This place looks great! I think we have a winner!

BAILEY: You said it! Hey, wait. What's this? Oh, no, a package from the folks!

ADAMS: I know. I can smell it.

BAILEY: Wow! That really stinks! You know, maybe we should open a fresh fish place down at the shore.

Host: And so, our friends opened their *first* business with much fanfare, publicity and great reviews! And yes, each of them owned a Ferrari!

Let's thank "Adams and Bailey" for their help!

But what happens when The Lord God enters into a blood covenant with an individual?

Guest: Why would The Lord God do that?

Guest: . . . because He needed a friend on earth . . .

Guest: . . . with whom He could cut a blood covenant of strong friendship . . .

Guest: . . . so that the "Someone" promised in the Garden of Eden could appear . . . .

Guest: He found that friend in Abraham.

Host: We see that Abraham, or Abram, as he was first called, met the Almighty God through a conversation that included a promise.

Over the next twenty-five years of Abram's life, God would explore His promises and His blood covenant with Abram.

If we could have two volunteers, we are going to see that many of the elements of the blood covenant between individuals were also present in this wonderful relationship between Almighty God and Abram.

So, let's set the stage. Abram lived with his wife, Sarai, and extended family in the sophisticated city of Ur. At some point in his life, a yearning began to stir in Abram's heart that there was something more to life than what he currently had.

And then one night:

THE LORD: Hey, Abram, wake up!

ABRAM: AHH! My tent's on fire!

THE LORD: Don't worry. It's the glory of Heaven!

ABRAM: That's amazing! And You are-

THE LORD: Almighty God. I came because I feel that you're looking for something more in life.

ABRAM: You're right! How did You know that?

THE LORD: Let's just say that I know lots of things. I know that you've been feeling "stuck" for some time now.

ABRAM: You understand about being stuck?

THE LORD: Sure I do! But I have something to help you out.

ABRAM: A set of new camels would be nice.

THE LORD: Ok. I think I can find you some good camels. But I was actually thinking of something else.

ABRAM: Like—

THE LORD: Like . . . some promises!

ABRAM: Promises? What kind of promises?

THE LORD: Oh, wonderful promises, Abram. I want you to know that I'm going to make you a great nation.

ABRAM: Umm . . . Lord, I don't mean to tell You how to run Your business, I mean my life, but You need *people* to make a great nation.

THE LORD: Precisely!

ABRAM: And grown people were once little kids . . .

THE LORD: Yes, I understand how that works . . .

ABRAM: And I don't have any kids that are going to grow up and make a great nation!

THE LORD: Oh, is that what you're worried about? Don't worry. That will all work out. Now, as I was saying, I'm going to bless you with a great life, full of health and treasures, fame and fortune. You know—the good life!

ABRAM: Wow!

THE LORD: Yep! People for ages and ages are going to remember the distinguished name and life of Abram. In fact, I'm going to bless everyone who blesses you and deal with those who don't. How does that sound?

ABRAM: It sounds like . . . like something out of this world! Thank You for including me in it.

THE LORD: Thank you for accepting. You see, I've got magnificent plans for you. In fact, through you every family of the earth shall be blessed!

ABRAM: Every family?

THE LORD: Every one of them!

ABRAM: That's an awesome promise . . . from an awesome God. You're not like the other gods. You're really special.

THE LORD: And so are you.

Host: From that time on a strong friendship began to develop between The Lord God and Abram.

Guest: Later, as a sign of that friendship, The Lord God sent a special visitor to Abram.

Guest: This visitor, Melchizedek, was a king and a priest of the Most High God.

Host: Melchizedek and Abram shared a covenant meal of bread and wine after Abram's victorious rescue of his nephew, Lot.

Guest: On Heaven's behalf, Melchizedek spoke blessings. On his family's behalf, Abram gave a tenth of all he had won in battle.

Guest: And why not? The Most High God, Who was the Owner of Heaven and earth, had fulfilled His promise of opening Heaven's treasury to him.

Guest: Giving him health and wealth, He had also given him victory over every enemy.

Host: So Abram lived in the blessings of God.

Guest: But "after these things," something happened in Abram's heart.

Guest: The years had passed, and one day Abram looked around his tent and said to himself:

ABRAM: What am I doing with my life?

THE LORD: Hey Abe, it's Me. Just wanted to let you know—Don't worry!

ABRAM: Ok, I'll try.

THE LORD: Please try. You know, you don't have to be afraid. I'm here with you and for you. I'm your Shield, and because you fought for Me and honored Me with your gifts, I'm going to give you great rewards.

ABRAM: Thanks, Lord. I really appreciate that. But there's just one thing.

THE LORD: Ask Me anything, My friend.

ABRAM: Does that reward include kids? I mean, I appreciate all the things You've given me, but I still feel kind of empty inside. When I'm gone, who will take care of everything You've given me?

THE LORD: Abe, come outside with Me.

ABRAM: It's nice out here . . . kinda stuffy in the tent.

THE LORD: Kinda limits your thinking in there, too! Now look up! Look toward heaven and count the stars, if you can. That's how many kids you're going to have!

ABRAM: Wow! That's a lot of stars!

THE LORD: That's a bunch of kids! You're going to need some land—how about this one?

ABRAM: Can I ask You something, Lord? You won't be mad, will You?

THE LORD: Of course not! I love a good conversation.

ABRAM: Did You make all those stars?

THE LORD: Sure did! I know all their names, too!

ABRAM: You named the stars?

THE LORD: Absolutely! Names are important, you know.

ABRAM: And this land . . . You can give it to me?

THE LORD: I sure can. Let's just say that it's been in My family, forever!

ABRAM: Great! Well, I just want to tell You that I believe in You, Who You are and what You say!

THE LORD: I believe in you, too, Abram, and I'm going to deposit your belief in Me into your heavenly account and mark it "righteousness."

ABRAM: "Righteous Abram" . . . who would have thought . . . there's just one more thing, Lord. Could You just guarantee this for me?

THE LORD: Abe, I see that there's only one thing to do. Go get Me the things on this list . . . .

Host: So, what do we see so far? The Lord and Abram had established a blood covenant of strong friendship.

The Lord and Abram exchanged their "outer clothing." Almighty God clothed Abram in the anointing of His

Spirit. Abram gave the Lord a blood covenant friend in the earth.

They also exchanged weapons. Abram and his allies conquered the power of evil kings and rescued Lot. The Lord gave Abram the Shield of His Presence.

They exchanged blessings over the covenant meal of bread and wine. The Most High God adopted Abram into his family. Abram gave The Lord a tenth of all that he had.

Guest: Still, Abram is concerned about the legacy he will leave behind.

Guest: The Almighty God told Abram to get five kinds of animals that represented offerings from all levels of society.

Guest: The Lord was about to enter into a special blood covenant with His friend who needed a little extra help in believing.

Host: Abram sacrificed the animals in blood covenant fashion, cutting them down the mid-line and laying the halves along either side of a center pathway.

Guest: The blood of the animals seeped into the ground as Abram waited for the Lord to appear.

Guest: Daylight came. The Lord did not.

Guest: The vultures arrived, instead.

Host: And so, in the waiting time, Abram fought off the physical vultures that attacked his sacrifices, and the mental vultures that attacked his faith.

Guest: And then, as the sun set, The Lord God appeared and put Abram into a "twilight sleep," so that his spirit could receive what his exhausted mind and body could not.

Guest: The glory of Heaven descended. The Lord God, as the smoking oven, and The Spirit of God, as the burning torch, walked between the blood covenant sacrifices.

Guest: They spoke promises to Abram concerning the land and his descendants, telling him of their sorrows and triumphs.

Host: Even more than this, They gave Abram an indelible picture of The Heavenly Family and Their interaction with earth. As The Lord God and The Holy Spirit walked through the pieces, They pointed to another member of Their family, One Who had been slain since before that blood-soaked land had been created.

Guest: The sacrificial animals represented That One, "That Someone" Who was to come.

Guest: The blood of those animals represented the blood of that Heavenly One.

Guest: Later, Abram would shed his blood as a mark of this blood covenant process.

Host: Only a few more steps lay between Abram and the fulfillment of the promise. The Lord God, therefore, took the next step.

THE LORD: Abram, I've got some good news for you. I'm going to change your name!

ABRAM: Change my name? I thought my name was famous and distinguished.

THE LORD: Oh, it is. But I know your heart's desire.

ABRAM: Oh, yes . . . so my new name is . . .

THE LORD: How does "Dad" sound? How do you like this? "Abraham, the father of many nations!" And We'll change Sarai's name, too: "Sarah, the mother of a multitude, the mother of kings!"

ABRAM: Wow!!! You have a sense of humor! I'm ninety-nine years old now, and Sarah's not far behind me, though she'd never admit it! How's this going to work, if I may ask?

THE LORD: Oh, Abraham, father of many nations! Is anything too hard or too wonderful for Me to do? Come on, let's go get some food, have a covenant meal, and seal our agreement. How does that sound?

ABRAM: Sounds great. I'll prepare the lamb, and Sarah's got a new cake recipe.

THE LORD: What are We waiting for? You, My friend, are about to enter the best days of your life!

Guest: The Lord kept His promise, and Abraham and Sarah did have a son, Isaac, whose name means "laughter."

Guest: The Lord *does* have a sense of humor, after all.

Guest: There is one final piece of the blood covenant: the test of the blood covenant relationship.

Host: The years passed, filled with the joys and happiness, the heartache and difficult decisions that are called "life" . . .

Guest: . . . until the day came that Abraham's Covenant Partner, the Almighty God, asked Abraham to give up the thing dearest to his heart: his only son, Isaac.

Guest: Abraham "rose early in the morning." He did not hesitate to begin his most difficult journey of faith.

Guest: But he moved in faith and spoke in faith.

Host: "Then on the third day Abraham lifted up his eyes, and saw the place afar off."

Guest: He saw a Cross on a jagged hill in a distant time, where another burnt offering would be given.

Guest: He saw a Father's agony. He saw a Son's suffering.

Guest: But he also saw a resurrection and a return home.

Host: So strengthened was his faith that he could say to his helpers: "I and the lad will go . . . and worship and come again to you."

Guest: So much strengthened that he could tell Isaac, "God will provide Himself a lamb for a burnt offering."

Guest: The Almighty God honored Abraham's faithful obedience, sparing Isaac by providing a "ram in the bush" instead.

Host: By doing so, Abraham gave The Lord God the final piece of His covenant: the rebirth and resurrection of *His* only begotten Son.

Guest: The Lord God summed it all up when He said: "By Myself have I sworn . . . that in blessing, I will bless you . . ."

Guest: And He added the good news of the blood covenant: ". . . and in your Descendant shall all the families of the earth be blessed."

Guest: "That Someone" promised in the Garden of Eden was on His way!

Painting the Picture

Host: As the ages rolled by, the angels realized that Heaven was painting a picture with words.

Guest: The Lord God spoke that Someone would come and conquer the enemy and all his forces.

Guest: . . . That Someone would come with the heavenly authority and compassion to rescue humanity.

Guest: . . . That Someone would come to open the way for every family on the earth to be blessed.

Host: . . . That Someone would be able to do this because He loved righteousness and detested wickedness.

Guest: Therefore, God, His God, would anoint Him with the oil of joy and gladness.

Guest: He was "a Star that would come out of Jacob . . ."

Guest: "The Dayspring from on high . . . The Dawn of a new day."

Host: Jacob called Him "Shiloh," the Prince of Peace, the One appointed heir of the world.

Guest: The prophets called Him "a great light."

Guest: ". . . a hiding place from the wind and a shelter from the tempest . . ."

Host: . . . One Who is like fire, shining with the brilliance of light, radiant as a rainbow.

Guest: John the Baptist saw Him when the Spirit of God descended and remained on Him.

Guest: Filled with awe, John exclaimed: "Behold, the Lamb of God who takes away the sin of the world!"

Host: This Lamb of God, Jesus of Nazareth, anointed with the Holy Spirit and with power, went about doing good and healing all who were tormented by the devil!

Guest: He was strong and able to do this, because God was with Him.

Guest: And so, three and a half years passed, filled with mercy and compassion, signs and wonders.

Host: But the moment arrived when Jesus knew that the time had come for the completion of a promise given in a Garden so long ago.

THAT SOMEONE

Host: Endings and beginnings can be difficult for people, Jesus reflected as He awakened early on His last day of freedom. Just a few days ago, many thought of My victorious entry into Jerusalem as the beginning of a national change, and yet it really was the signal for the end of an era.

He arose in the darkness and made His way to the door.

No need to disturb His weary disciples or His host, Lazarus, from their much needed rest.

The house had a quiet stillness about it, as if it had shaken off the mourners who had come to comfort His dear friends, Martha and Mary . . . the curious who had come to peek at Lazarus, newly risen from the dead . . . the steady stream of pilgrims on the Jericho road that wound past Bethany on the way to Jerusalem.

Guest: Yes, He thought, this house has been the place of gentle memories, of uncontested devotion, of that special quality called . . . home.

Host: He reached the door, opened it and stepped into the garden, which offered to Him its fragrances of cinnamon and aloe, frankincense and spikenard.

Guest: Spikenard, He reminisced, that spikenard treasured in an alabaster box, yet last night was poured on My head through sorrow-filled tears . . . anointing Me for My death and burial . . .

Guest: . . . a burial that would be made in haste . . .

Host: . . . and so wonderful Holy Spirit inspired a friend who loves Me to prepare My body for the grave . . . even though I'll only be there three days and three nights.

But those days . . . those days will close an age, a piece of time that will never return . . . Those days will open a time that will last forever . . . My Kingdom . . . the Kingdom of the Son whom the Father loves . . .

He had reached the fig trees that grew in the garden, their green figs and budding leaves enjoying the warmth of the soft wind that floated around them.

Guest: A tree . . . a garden . . . simple things that will change My life . . .

Guest: . . . forever, He whispered to the morning light.

Guest: Yes, all was in place. The Passover would begin this evening.

Guest: A time of celebration . . . the remembrance of blood covenant promises that brought pardon and rescue and freedom.

Guest: Who realized, He thought, that in the midst of this joyous festival a new way was being built?

Guest: Yes, *I* am the Way back to Father . . . to light and life . . . to happiness and all that is good.

Host: He had reached a small clearing through which a narrow path led to the outer wall of the garden.

Guest: How like the road that lies before Me.

Guest: Yes, Father, all the appropriate steps will be finished . . .

Guest: They'll exchange My clothing, crowning Me as "King", yet I will feel like "tola," a worm crushed so that its precious hidden riches may flow out.

Host: My friends will try to fight with the sword, but My sword will be Your Word.

Guest: And the blood . . .

Guest: . . . of the Passover lambs, yes, those innocent ones whose blood had been sprinkled, whose bodies had been roasted in fire, to save from wrath, to cover sin . . .

Guest: But now My own blood, the blood of God's Lamb, will forever take away the sin of the world.

Host: He approached a small cluster of palm trees whose presence brought relief from the rising heat. He sat, reclining against the cool trunk of the tree.

Guest: No more lambs to the Temple, Father; No more rituals of sacrifice, are there, Holy Spirit?

Host: The Father's Lamb is here, the last sacrifice for sin, forever.

Guest: And when this "veil" of My flesh is torn, when My blood is sprinkled before the heavenly altar, the wall that separates people from Heaven and from each other will be gone.

Host: The muffled voices of straggling travelers, the thud of their donkeys' hooves as they went by, broke into His thoughts.

He rose, leaving the comforting shade of the palm trees.

Another tree awaits Me, but after that . . . after that price has been paid and the victory has been won, there awaits . . .

Guest: . . . the joy and the glory that I once knew in Heaven with My Father.

Host: He turned to leave, allowing the strength of that memory to seep into His soul.

Guest: What a wondrous mystery lives in gardens, He thought.

Guest: I remember it so well . . . in a garden I became the Lamb slain before the foundation of the world . . . a garden where My Father promised that Someone would come and crush the head of the enemy . . . a garden where death will soon almost overwhelm Me . . . a garden where My resurrection life will begin its never-ending flow.

Host: He was back at the house, where the night's stillness had given way to the busyness of the day.

The familiar voices of His friends called to Him, "where should we go and prepare the Passover?"

He answered them, and a flood of love and tenderness rose from a deep secret place in His soul.

"Yes," He whispered, "go and get the guest chamber ready, for God has prepared Himself a Lamb."

"The Lord's Passover is ready."

THE BREAD AND THE WINE (THE SEDER)

The Lighting of the Candles

Guest: We love You, Father.

              We love You, Jesus.

              We love You, Holy Spirit.

Family: We open our hearts to receive Your holy Presence.

[The host fills the Cup of Elijah and says: "We fill this Cup of Elijah to show that Jesus Christ is here with us!"]

Introduction

Host: Jesus of Nazareth took His place as the host of the evening's supper. Knowing that soon He would become the last Passover lamb, He lifted up the Cup of Sanctification with the hope and faith that, in the retelling of this story, they would see the eternal Lamb of God.

The First Cup: Sanctification

[The first cups are filled.]

[The host lifts his cup and says:]

Host: Once we and our ancestors were without hope and without God in this world.

Family: But now by the sacrifice of Himself, Jesus has purged away our sins, by forgiving all the wrong things we have thought and done.

Guest: He has done this so that we may have a life of eternal closeness to The Father by the Holy Spirit.

Host: Thank You, Jesus, for cleansing us from all unrighteousness.
           Let us drink the cup of sanctification.

[Everyone drinks the first cup.]

The Washing of the Hands

[The host washes his hands and says]:

Host: In the book of Exodus, the priests in Israel were commanded to wash their hands and their feet before entering the Presence of God.

           Jesus knew that soon the Holy Spirit's Presence would flood creation with power that had never before been seen.

           This time a kingdom of kings and priests would rise up in worship, in signs and in wonders.

           They needed to know that they had been cleansed and filled with the authority of Heaven.

           Therefore, Jesus took off his outer coat, put on the apron of a servant, and washed His disciples' feet.

Family: Now we, as His followers, wash each other's hands to show that our lives are cleansed by His word.

[Each person takes a towelette and washes another person's hands.]

Song (optional)

The Parsley and the Salt Water

[Everyone takes two pieces of parsley and dips them, one at a time, into the salt water.]

Host: The first piece of parsley represents the tears shed by Abraham's descendants when they were in slavery.

Like them we cried sorrowful tears when the chains of sin and death held us in bondage.

[Everyone eats the first piece of parsley.]

Family: The second piece of parsley shows the tears of joy when the Lord rescued them with a mighty hand and carried them on eagles' wings.

Guest: We, too, rejoice because He has rescued us from the kingdom of darkness, and placed us into the kingdom of His Beloved Son.

[Everyone eats the second piece of parsley.]

The Breaking of the Middle Matzah

[The host breaks the middle matzah, leaving one half between the remaining whole matzahs.]

Host: Everyone has to close their eyes! And no peeking!

[He hides the broken half of matzah.]

Host: This hidden matzah is called the "Afikomen." Once it is found, I will explain its secret!

The Re-telling of the Story of Passover and the Exodus

Host: The original Passover story is filled with magnificent wonders, founded on acts of faith, and concluded with majestic praise.

Guest: And, although this story concerns the Israelites, each of us has a part in it.

Guest: It is for those who have grown weary.

Guest: It is for those whose future seems hidden, out of reach, and far away.

Guest: It is for those who desire true freedom and real victory in their lives.

Guest: It is a story of rescue.

Guest: It is a story of miracles.

Host: It is The Lord's Passover.

The Second Cup: The Cup of Plagues

[The second cups are filled.] [Everyone prepares a mixture of matzah, bitter herbs and charoseth.]

Youngest: Can you tell us, please, about the Lord's Passover?

Host: Sure, I'd love to. Do you remember when the Lord God cut the covenant with Abraham, and He moved among the pieces as a smoking oven and a burning lamp?

Youngest: Yes, I do.

Host: During that time when the Father and The Holy Spirit walked through the blood of the animals, the Father told Abraham that his descendants would be slaves for four hundred years and would then be rescued.

Youngest: That's a really long time.

Host: It sure is. For four hundred years Abraham's descendants, the family of Jacob, lived in the land of Egypt.

Guest: Many years were happy years because the Pharaoh and the Egyptians thought well of Jacob.

Guest: They were grateful for Jacob's son, Joseph, who had helped them during a time of great famine, when food was hard to find.

Guest: But after Pharaoh and Joseph's generation passed away, another king arose who did not remember the good things that Joseph and his God had done for them.

Guest: Times became hard for them, and Joseph's family fell from wealth into slavery.

Host: So, let's eat this a mixture of the matzah, bitter herbs, and charoseth, and we'll continue the story.

[Everyone eats.]

Youngest: Please tell us why we eat this?

Host: Yes, I'd love to. Thanks for asking! The Lord God wanted them to eat this so that they would remember that He keeps His blood covenant promises.

Youngest: How did eating help them to remember?

Host: That's a great question. Maybe it's because we remember what we eat, how it tastes and how it makes us feel.

Guest: The bitter herbs reminded them of the bitter affliction of slavery.

Guest: For us, too, it reminds us that bitterness and sorrow grow in a life that follows sin and rejoices in death.

Guest: The charoseth reminded them of the straw and mortar that they had used in making bricks for a cruel king.

Guest: For us it reminds us to build our lives on the great rock called Jesus, not on the "bricks" of pride and self-conceit.

Guest: The matzah, which was bread that did not have time to rise, reminded them that their God was able to rescue them with quickness and power.

Guest: For us, too, God is a mighty and miraculous God Who works—suddenly!

Youngest: . . . like really fast!

Host: Really fast! Now this is the thing about God that sometimes is hard to understand. He has a heavenly calendar that may not always match with our timing.

Youngest: Okay. So that means . . . what *does* that mean?

Guest: That means that sometimes it *feels* like God is taking a long time to answer His promises!

Host: But He makes all things beautiful just at the right time!

Guest: And when that time comes, all of a sudden, God moves!

Youngest: So God looked at His calendar and saw it was time to move!

Guest: Exactly! He moved because something special happened on earth.

Youngest: What was that?

Guest: The children of Israel prayed.

Youngest: Did that help?

Host: Most certainly! Believe me, any prayer that comes from your heart means something to God. He sent Moses, a man of prayer and faith, to help them.

Youngest: How could one person help so many people?

Host: He helped them by encouraging them to believe and obey the Lord God's instructions.

Guest: He told them to take a one-year old male lamb from their flocks, one that was perfect and without blemish.

Guest: On the tenth day of the month, this special lamb was chosen.

Guest: Each family was to have a lamb . . . a lamb for a family . . . no one who was part of Abraham's descendants, or who had been marked with the covenant of Abraham, was to be left out.

Guest: At twilight on the fourteenth day, every Israelite household was to slay the lamb and put its blood on the top and two sides of the doorpost of their houses.

Host: Then they roasted the body of the lamb and ate it. None of it was left until morning, and none of its bones were broken.

[The host lifts the lamb bone.]

Host: This lamb bone represents the Passover lambs whose innocent lives were given to spare the lives of Jacob's family.

Guest: Then they had to stay inside until morning!

Youngest: They couldn't play outside?

Host: Not on that night! At midnight the angel of death came to search the land. Any house that did not have the blood of the lamb on its doorpost, he was able to enter. But wherever the lamb's blood had been applied, he was not allowed to go in, for the lamb's blood brought the Lord God's glory to that place. He had to "pass over" that house.

Therefore, the lamb and its blood became the Lord's Passover.

Youngest: Thank God for all the Passover lambs!!!

Host: That's right! Hallelujah! Now we can rejoice because Jesus is our Passover Lamb!

Guest: He is perfect and sinless.

Guest: His Body was torn apart during His suffering.

Guest: His blood was put on the doorposts of a wooden Cross at Calvary.

Guest: Yet none of His bones were broken.

Host: He gave His innocent life to spare our lives from the punishment of sin.

Family: Thank You, Father, for Jesus Christ, our Passover Lamb!

[Everyone lifts up the second cup while the Host says]:

Host: We live in Your Presence, Father, because of Jesus, our Passover Lamb. Now no evil befalls us. No plague, calamity, or accident comes near our dwellings, because You have given Your angels charge over us!

[Everyone drinks the second cup.]

The Roasted Egg

[The roasted egg is lifted and the host says]:

Host: This egg, which symbolizes the never-ending newness of life, reminds us that we are a new creation, walking in the peace and mercy of God.

The Search for the Afikomen

[A search for the hidden matzah occurs. When it is found it is shared with all.]

[The host washes his hands and lifts up the three matzahs.]

Host: These three matzahs represent God the Father, Jesus the Son, and God The Holy Spirit. These Three are One.

The middle matzah represents our Lord Jesus Christ, Whose body was broken in death to pay for our sins.

The Afikomen is found and shared to show that we, too, can find and share the resurrection life of Jesus Christ.

The Third Cup: The Cup of Blessing

[The third cups are filled.]

Host: The moment had come—written in the glory of eternity past, then hidden for a time to come.

Guest: And now that time was here . . .

Guest: . . . that moment when the Father's cry reached Jesus' heart: "Please bring Our family home."

Guest: His thoughts moved across His days on earth . . . the healings . . . the eyes that saw, the ears that heard, the lips that spoke, the minds that were calmed . . . the love that was there . . .

Guest: Yes, He thought, I have shown the Father to His children.

Guest: Yes, as I told My friend, Philip, "He who has seen Me has seen the Father."

Guest: One final step remained . . .

Host: . . . to bring the children back to their Father.

Guest: But a bill of unpaid sin stood before Him.

Guest: An interest penalty for guilt and lawlessness loomed ahead . . .

Guest: . . . and a punishment and chastisement that would bring peace to others called Him forward.

Guest: A debt, made by ancestors long ago, had now become due.

Host: Its payment will cost Me everything, He thought, as He reached for the third cup.

Even now it has begun. Judas, once my friend, has now become My betrayer. And these who are left do not understand the separation that is to come.

Guest: And yet Holy Spirit is bringing the fire of Heaven into My soul . . . The One who led Me into the wilderness, the One who infused Me with power . . .

Guest: The Holy Spirit who descended like a dove into My life, now ignites the fire of Heaven within My Spirit.

Guest: Drawing strength from this inner gift, He spoke over the third cup, the Cup of Blessing, saying: "This cup is the new covenant in My blood, which is shed for the remission of sins."

Guest: Father, I pray that they understand the fullness of this blessing; that they are whole; that all is well.

Host: Father, let them live in Your love. Let them see the glory that You gave Me before time existed.

Guest: This Afikomen, the broken bread, tells them of My death. This cup tells them that the life of My blessing is being transferred to them.

Host: Let us drink this cup of blessing and receive our inheritance of peace, prosperity, and health, for everything that involves true life and godliness is now ours.

[Everyone drinks the third cup.]

Song

Gethsemane

Host: Descending the steps from the upper chamber, we sang a Hymn, the sounds of the last Hallels lingering in the festive night air.

Then it came.

The change began at the Kidron, that brook of sorrow and mourning, its swollen winter rains flowing like tears from past generations.

Yes, Jesus thought, a change has come. The air has changed, for now I sense the presence of one who has found his opportune time.

Guest: He quickened His steps, the pounding of His heart providing the cadence which His feet followed.

Guest: The singing of His friends had ceased, the words lost in their attempt to keep pace with Him.

Guest: Climbing the lower western slope of Mt. Olivet, they entered the garden of the olive press.

Guest: On all other nights, the soothing solitude of the fruit and olive trees welcomed Him.

Guest: But this night's quietness had been dissolved by an agitation of spirit that gnawed within His soul.

Guest: . . . for this Passover night *was* different from all other nights.

Host: Tonight, He thought as He passed beside the olive press building, tonight My countrymen rejoice . . .

rejoice because the blood of the lambs stopped the angel of death . . . rejoice because their first-born sons live, protected by that blood . . . rejoice because they escaped the land of bondage.

Guest: But tonight this garden has become the place where the death angel prowls, and I have become the first born whom he desires to kill.

Guest: He stopped, as if in doing so the flow of thoughts would stop also.

Guest: Turning, He motioned for His disciples to join Him.

Guest: Those who had been so close, now with frightened eyes, followed at a distance.

Host: What are we to do, their eyes asked, searching His face for its familiar strength and confident ease.

Guest: What is there to do, His eyes responded, when night comes and no man can work?

Guest: Pray, His eyes replied, for no time remained for a spoken explanation.

Host: When night comes, what is there to do but pray?

           Motioning for His three closest friends, He moved toward a clearing among the trees.

           "May these three who have seen My glory, help Me through My sorrow," He whispered.

Guest: Their sluggish eyes and drooping shoulders suggested otherwise, and a realization grew . . .

Guest: . . . sorrow-filled friends . . . the silence of Heaven . . . the terror that startles My soul . . .

Host: "I am alone," He whispered as He fell on His face in prayer.

At one time My Father was close to Me, My friends were beside Me, He thought.

But that was before I crossed the Kidron.

Guest: Another was with Him now.

Guest: "The one who had found the wound in Judas' soul is probing to find the wound in Mine."

Guest: The heartbeats came faster now, short and quick . . .

Guest: The breathing, sharp and stifled by the heaviness of the night air that refused to offer its flow.

Host: But Heaven had released a cup to Him.

"Drink," Heaven said.

Drink, He thought. Tonight I gave My disciples the cup of the New Covenant. But for them to truly drink that cup, I must drink this one . . .

Sorrow's cup . . . the cup of permission to become the one who carries the guilt of the world into the abyss of death . . . to become the scapegoat . . . the one without a future, without the hope of redemption . . . for I give that redemption to My friends and to the world . . .

Guest: The terror of death stabbed His soul again, piercing it with mocking threats of eternal separation . . . of being cut off forever from the love of Heaven.

Guest: "My Abba, My Abba," He cried, "if it is possible, let this hour, let this cup pass from Me."

Guest: The chains of death are swirling, wrapping themselves around the pillars of My soul, choking off every whispered hope, every joyous memory.

Guest: And now I must fight against the sweet velvet darkness that coaxes me to come and rest . . . to enter the rest of death . . .

Guest: "My Abba, My Abba, let this cup pass from Me . . ."

Host: The darkness is calling Me, but a glow of light is rising and in that glow a word . . .

"Nevertheless . . ."

Guest: "Nevertheless"—because I always do those things that please My Father.

Guest: "Nevertheless" . . . because it pleases the Father to see the victory from the travail of My soul . . . that many will come home to glory, come home to be with Us.

Guest: Nevertheless, not My will, but forever Your will is what I desire.

Host: A soft wind swirled around Him in a gentle embrace. An angel from Heaven appeared, giving Him the strength to reject the invitation of death.

Guest: But another voice now asserted itself, with screams of accusations and howls of jeering laughter.

Guest: Another voice, that voice of doubt from an ancient garden, now began to encircle His mind, pounding it with tightening pressure.

Guest: "If You are the Son of God . . . if You are . . . then why . . ."

Host: The agony . . . the accusations . . . the pressures . . . assailed Him.

          The tears seeped from His eyes, the sweat flowed from His forehead. He felt it travel down His face and drop to the ground. Opening His eyes, He saw that it was blood . . .

          "My blood," He whispered.

Guest: The howls of laughter erupted again, rising on a flood of new accusations.

Guest: "If You are the Son of God, then . . ."

          "If You had listened to me in the wilderness . . ."

          "If You had accepted my offer to be King back then . . . ."

          ". . . But look at You now . . . rejected . . . alone . . . and unloved."

Host: No! Not true! That's a lie . . . a lie!

          "I am the Son of His love; My Father *does* love me. I am coming to do Your will, My Abba," Jesus whispered.

Guest: The words began to rise, like dew that faces the morning sun . . .

Host: "Someone is coming to crush the head of the serpent . . . Someone to bless all the families of the earth . . . Someone to bring the children home to Heaven."

Guest: His breathing slowed, and the waves of accusations receded.

Guest: "Yes," He continued, rising from the ground. "In the volume of the Book, it is written of Me—'I delight to do Your will' . . . I always do the things that please You."

Host: He rose to His feet, and thanking His Father for a peace that was beyond earthly comprehension, He walked over to His sleeping disciples.

The Crucifixion

Host: The moments tumbled over one another . . . the soldiers' violence . . . the mob's anger . . . the accusations of those in authority . . .

The heavens are being shaken, He thought, shaken for the birth of the covenant in My blood. A birth that leads through the Cross.

My Lord, hear me in this day of My trouble . . .

Do not be far from Me . . . where I cannot reach You with My prayers . . .

I call to You, but there is no answer . . .

I call and am not silent . . .

Trouble is near, and everyone is far away . . .

I lay here in this dust of death, as godless men pierce My hands and My feet.

I lay here, dying, as evil men swirl around Me like wolves entrapping their prey . . .

Guest: Father, forgive them, for they don't realize what they are doing.

Guest: They see Me, and with mocking laughter, they scorn the trust that I have in You.

Guest: They say that You have abandoned Me, because You have not come to rescue Me.

Host: Still . . . I hear words of faith from a nearby cross—

I turn my head toward him, despite the searing pain of the thorns . . . the nails . . . the wounds . . .

Guest: "Jesus, remember me when You come into Your kingdom."

Host: "Today, My friend, you shall be with Me in paradise."

" Yes, I will leave you in Father Abraham's arms, but I . . ."

Guest: I am a worm, crushed by the weight of generations of sin . . . bruised and crimson by its devouring power.

Guest: But even in this, I know what the scornful do not know . . . that this broken Man who will become sin, is in truth Heaven's scarlet thread; like the one that hung in Rahab's window, a blood covenant symbol of a promised rescue.

Guest: O My Father, may they believe Me and the promises I have spoken. For I have trusted You, even when I was young and held in My mother's arms.

Host: And now I see the tears that spill from her sword-pierced soul . . . tears that have been stored for many years, My God.

Guest: I watch . . . I watch My friend comfort her, holding her as I would do, if I could . . .

"Dear woman,
Look, here is your son."

"My friend,
Look, here is your mother."

Guest: My heart is melting away, collapsing with every beat. No longer do My bones join together, but like softened wax, My life is oozing out of Me.

Guest: But My mother will do well. My friends and brothers will come to a lasting faith.

Guest: And with much joy and great love, I will see My kingdom filled with kings and priests who appreciate the bloodshed of My sacrifice.

Guest: But now darkness covers the land, and in that darkness a swirling wind sweeps across the heavens and calls to the four winds of the earth.

Guest: The furious wrath of God gathers sin and iniquity, poverty and disease from every moment of time . . .

Host: Reaching back to the most ancient moments, stretching out until time will be no more, and bringing each present breath, the wind storm of God funnels into Me the sin of humanity. On the Cross I have now become sin—
        "My God,
        My God,
        Why have You forsaken Me?"

Guest: Indeed, He has hidden His face from me, for a moment; for I have become the final sacrifice for sin.

Guest: But I know My Father. In His mercy, He will bring Me back to Him again.

Guest: The veil of the Temple that enclosed the Most Holy Place has been torn from the top to the bottom—from Heaven down to earth.

Guest: The glorious mercy of My Father flows out to everyone.

Host: So now I can speak the prophetic words "I thirst" . . . for righteousness, love, and mercy; knowing that My family can drink and never thirst again.

The battlefield of Calvary, which began with My seeming defeat, has now become My overwhelming victory.

"It is finished," I proclaim to Heaven and earth.

My Father is by My side once again.

"Father, into Your hands I commit My spirit."

My work on earth is complete.

I pour My soul into death and take My last breath.

The Burial

Guest: As evening approached, there came a rich man from Arimathea, named Joseph, who had himself become a disciple of Jesus.

                    Going to Pilate, he asked for Jesus' body . . .

                    He took the body, wrapped it in clean linen cloths and placed it in his own new tomb that he had cut out of the rock.

                    He rolled a big stone in front of the entrance to the tomb and went away.

The Descent

Host: My work in the belly of the earth, however, had just begun.

I descended with the others who had died on that day.

The earth, in layers of unwinding circles, opened to receive us.

An angel led the way, carrying a bright flaming torch.

Some who were descending were escorted by angels who carried smaller torches, which bathed each person in shimmering pools of light.

Those without angelic escorts still moved along in quiet hopefulness . . . hopeful, for we descended toward the soft glow of lighted arches which floated in the surrounding darkness.

We stopped there as the leading angel approached the entrance gate.

A distinguished man emerged (whom I recognized as Father Abraham) and greeted the angel who then handed him a scroll.

Each escort angel then presented the person over whom he had been given charge to Father Abraham.

When My friend, once a thief, now a just man, stepped into the threshold of Paradise, he turned and waited for Me, expecting Me to join him.

I nodded to him in appreciation and watched in gratitude as his escort angel delivered him into Father Abraham's arms.

He would now join them as they waited in faith for salvation.

Our descent began again, this time into unrelenting darkness.

Although Paradise was a haven for those who had lived in righteous faith, it became the first step in a torturous descent for those who had not!

Torturous—for it revealed to the condemned what might have been.

Only once before (as Our adversary fell from Heaven) have I heard such howls of despair, such shrieks of fear.

Never before have I heard such voices of remorse calling on the Name of the LORD, as they fell in unhindered descent.

The mocking thief from Calvary tumbled by without recognizing Me.

His mouth still spit out curses, but now they were mingled with frustrated and frightened pleas for "someone" to rescue him.

My last view of him was of a man twisted in anguish and chained in despair.

His shrieks became fainter; drowned out by the cries of those in the darkened torture that cycled toward eternity.

The demon jailers who now escorted us snarled in derision, singing their hideous song: ". . . too late for you, too late for me, too late for everyone you see . . ."

Other aspects of My descent I will not share at this time. There are appointed times of revelation and chosen times of silence.

But these thoughts I can leave with you.

On the Cross I was the Lamb of God Whose blood washed away the sin of the world.

In My descent I became the scapegoat, the one who carried a people's sin into the abyss, and out of sight—forever.

Guest: For you see, My soul, like My body, was made an offering for sin. The heaviness of sin, humanity's sin on Me, became like iron chains drawn by a magnet into the darkness of the earth.

Guest: This pull of the abyss stirred the depths of the earth to surge around Me and open wide, like the mouth of a devouring lion.

Guest: The traps of death swallowed Me, snapping shut as they hissed the word "forever" and closed behind Me.

Host: The torments of life among the dead I will not discuss.

Let it be enough to say that I came here, so that you would not have to do so.

I endured because hidden within My sin-infested and tormented soul were words . . . promises from ancient ages . . . sealed in the Blood . . . honored by Heaven.

Guest: . . . You shall crush the enemy's head . . .

Guest: This I have done on the Cross. Although he does not yet recognize his fatal wound, this I know:

Guest: . . . that My body lies in safety . . . that My spirit rejoices . . .

Guest: Why? Because My Father will not abandon Me in this place of death . . .

Guest: . . . Holy Spirit will show Me the path of life . . . the way of escape . . .

Guest: . . . And in doing so, *I* will become the path of life and way of escape for all those whose hearts yearn to be with My Father.

Guest: . . . In faith I saw what My soul's suffering would accomplish, and I was satisfied, for My Father's house would be full!

Guest: . . . therefore, in that place of torment and indignity, I shouted praises to My Father! A shout that rose from the inner depths of My soul; erupting with the force of a volcano, long thought dead, but revealing its strength and life.

Guest: My voice rang through the corridors of Hades . . . coursed through Paradise . . . and rose to the Highest Heaven.

Guest: It reached My Father's throne.

Guest: My blood, which was waiting in Heaven for Me, waiting to be sprinkled in that Most Holy Place, began to speak . . .

Guest: . . . to speak of resurrection and grace . . . of mercy and redemption . . .

Host: My Father rose from His throne, lifted His hand in solemn oath, and declared:

Jesus, My Son Whom I love, ARISE!!

Guest: His word swirled through the universe, marshalling Heaven's angelic forces, harnessing the winds, gathering the storm clouds.

Guest: Then Holy Spirit rode on the cherub, as the whirling wheels skimmed the four winds of the earth. A canopy of clouds surrounded Him, hiding His approach.

Guest: And suddenly . . . the sound... the fragrance . . . the mighty wind of Heaven invaded the atmosphere . . .

Guest: . . . and Holy Spirit appeared.

Host: The wind of Heaven, that majestic whirlwind encircled Me, and flung from My soul, every trace, every grasping tentacle of humanity's sin.

Then the holy fire of Heaven swept through the fibers of My soul, the lattice-work of My Being, purifying and reviving.

The eternal life of God, My Father's life, that glorious life flowed into Me, like melted sunshine. And I, Jesus the Christ, was born again as the resurrected Son of Man, as the Eternal Son of God.

Hallelujah!

Hallelujah!

Hallelujah!

Guest: I now surveyed the tragedy of hell with the eyes of Heaven.

Guest: What I saw, what I knew, brought fury to My soul, and fire in My Spirit.

Guest: Clothed once more in the armor of righteousness, I marched out, seeking to settle an ancient injustice which had been inflicted on Heaven and on humanity.

Host: I had conquered his domain, and I wanted him to know it . . . to know that a person filled with the Spirit of God was stronger than the traps of death.

Guest: No longer could sin and death terrorize those who belonged to Me.

Guest: I found him, that old serpent, the dragon, the adversary of all that is good, of all that is God.

Guest: I said, "I love righteousness, and hate lawlessness and iniquity."

Guest: "Therefore, My God has anointed Me with the oil of joy, and given me the scepter of righteousness, of authority."

Guest: So now—who is My adversary? Who will fight against Me?

Host: The dragon roared, as flickering sparks of fire and dust-filled profanities rolled from His mouth.

           It did not matter.

           His defeat had already been secured when I hung on the Cross. He knew it, and so did I.

           I stood there as a memorial that I had conquered every realm of existence.

           "I AM Jesus, Who was dead, and am now alive," I proclaimed.

           "And I live forevermore! Amen."

           As I spoke, the flaming, lightning-filled sword of Heaven appeared before Me.

           Stretching out My right hand, I reached through the flames and held its hilt.

           I marched toward him, My sword extended, flashes of glory surrounding Me.

He lunged, tried to encircle Me, and called his special warriors against Me. Although he attempted to hide behind the dusty soot of his foul breath, My eyes, with the clarity of holiness, saw beyond this.

I pierced the dragon, and with quick, precise strokes, stripped him of his unholy armor. Amid the shrieks and tormented screams of his followers, he deflated, sinking into the ground. His forces dispersed, running in fear and scattering into the darkness.

The lower region fell silent. I strode over to him and took his last possession from him.

"And I have the keys of death and hell," I declared.

The praises of those in Paradise erupted in waves of glorious shouts. My heavenly angels joined in, shouting with victorious voices that had waited for centuries for this moment.

I rose, walking through the sacred pathway constructed by the holy angels.

Suddenly—all the shouts of victory, all the words of praise, coalesced into one word:

"JESUS!"

I lifted My hands in praise to My Father and Holy Spirit, and in thanks to all those who had helped Me fulfill My Father's dream!

The Resurrection

Host: Escorted by My angels, I entered Paradise, where I was surrounded by relatives and friends.

Guest: We laughed and rejoiced, danced and sang, as I proclaimed the greatness of My Father's Name.

Guest: "My trust and confidence has always been in Him," I said.

Guest: I stood for a moment, soaking in the rejoicing. "And look," I continued, "here I am, I and the family Whom He has given Me."

Host: There was one family member I needed to find. I did. He was rejoicing, not with loud shouts of victory, but with tears and sobs, and hands lifted to Heaven.

He saw Me approach, and pressing through the crowd, came and bowed at My feet.

I kneeled down in front of him, placing My hand on his right shoulder.

Guest: He whispered, "I am the thief on the cross . . ."

Guest: I stood, and holding out My hand to him, helped him to his feet.

Guest: "No," I replied, "You were the voice of faith in My time of trouble. And now you are My brother."

Host: As the praises of Paradise erupted again, I shouted to everyone, "There's a place in My Kingdom waiting for each one of you!"

Host: Now Paradise can release into Heaven's care those whom it has protected in these past ages.

         Now the way to Heaven is open, for I am the Way. And I assure you of this: No matter how wonderful Paradise has been, Heaven is *so* much better!

Guest: In the darkness that lingered before the first rays of dawn, I re-entered the tomb of My burial.

Guest: How different this entrance was. The power of resurrection glory flowed through My soul, infusing it with heavenly zoë life.

Guest: That life was so powerful that the very substance of My body flooded through the grave clothes, unraveled the head cloth, and caused Me to stand in new life: a reborn spirit in a resurrected body, filled with the glory of God! Hallelujah!

Guest: The glorious wounds of My suffering still remain. But they are scars of honor, scars of love, the mark of the Blood Covenant.

Guest: They are the sign that I am a Covenant Man—forever joined to humanity . . .

Guest: . . . forever committed to them and to the promises made long ago in an eternal garden . . .

Guest: . . . the sign that those who believe in Me will always be whole and victorious, walking in the power of an endless life.

Guest: These wounds are the signal to all that because of My suffering, I am "That Someone" through Whom every family of the earth can now be blessed.

Guest: I smiled because My helper angels who had brought Me new clothes, did not quite understand Me. To see the power of Heaven wrapped in a resurrected body was a new revelation to them.

Host: . . . and to Me also . . .

Walking through the rock wall of the grave [one of My angels would soon roll away the stone], I passed the guards from whom I was hidden, and headed toward the quietness of the nearby garden.

Guest: I waited for the sunrise, for I wanted to know what it was like to be a citizen of Heaven who could still walk the earth.

Guest: But I heard the soft sobs of a broken heart, and I turned to find Mary of Magdala.

Guest: To her I entrusted the good news of the covenant, which I would soon to seal in My blood . . .

Guest: . . . that people can find rest; can find love and be loved in the arms of their Heavenly Father . . .

Guest: . . . that they can devote themselves, without fear, to a Father Who loves them, to the true and the Living God . . .

Host: Then I left, for My chariot of the whirling wheels had arrived, making the earth quake, and opening the tombs of the newly risen saints.

The angelic hosts lined the path of life, and Holy Spirit rode beside Me.

I was on My way home!

The Ascension

Host: I ascended to My Father, and entering the gates, I passed through the streets.

Multitudes of angels bowed in hushed adoration as I went by. I was overwhelmed. They had known Me as the Word Who was from the beginning.

Guest: Yet now they see Me—I am the Word Who was made flesh; the Son of God, the Son of Man . . .

Guest: . . . the One with wounded hands, marked brow and scarred feet . . . feet that carry Me up the steps into the Most Holy Place of All.

Guest: Taking the holy vessel that contains My blood, I entered the Most Holy Place, which had waited through the ages for the Resurrected Son of God to appear.

Guest: I came and took My place as High Priest, sprinkling My blood on the mercy seat of Heaven, which rests between the overshadowing cherubim.

Guest: With that sprinkling, I put away and destroyed the power of sin over humanity, because I Myself had become the final sacrifice for sin—forever!

Guest: With the sprinkling of My blood, eternal redemption was purchased for anyone who would receive.

Host: Then the glory in My blood met the Shekinah glory of Heaven. The smoke, fragrant with Heaven's anointing, filled the Temple with rolling waves of golden, billowy clouds!

Guest: As I emerged from these clouds of glory, My Father and Holy Spirit joined Me.

Guest: And now, once again at the rising of a new day, God and humanity stood together in love and holiness, in righteousness and redemption.

Guest: Then the festivities began as My Father proclaimed once again, "Let all the angels of God worship Him."

And they did. Their adoration from that day lives as an eternal memorial to their joy at My Homecoming.

Guest: Then Holy Spirit clothed Me in My robe of righteousness.

Host: My Father placed a crown upon My head, and a scepter of authority in My hand.

Then He decreed, "Your throne, O God, is forever!"

Guest: In truth and reality, I became the King of Kings and the Lord of Lords!

Guest: Soon I returned and spoke to My earthly friends. I taught and comforted, and explained My kingdom to them.

Guest: But Another would soon be sent . . . The Holy Spirit, Who would remain with them forever, ensuring that they are forever blessed!

Guest: One Who would lead and guide them into all truth; Who would show them things to come . . .

Guest: . . . Who would comfort, strengthen, and love them; just as I would do if I could be with each one of them.

Host: So—what do I leave you?

Oh, so many things . . . but put quite simply . . . I leave you the Covenant in My blood . . . the Covenant that was born out of the Cup of Blessing . . . the Covenant that was symbolized by the Afikomen, the broken bread, My broken body.

Guest: I leave you the assurance that this Covenant in My blood is now, and forever will be, in force . . .

Guest: It is unbreakable because My Father, Holy Spirit, and I always agree. We are one.

Guest: It is unchangeable, unaffected by circumstances and time.

Guest: We are not mortal. We have no need to lie. What We have promised We will do, and you will see, when you mix your faith with Our words.

Guest: We have clothed you in Our righteousness, and have given you heavenly weapons, mighty and powerful . . . able to overcome all opposition. We are not afraid of the adversary, neither should you be.

Guest: We have given you the Name of Jesus. Use it. Always remember the blood of the Covenant. Apply it! It was given for you.

Guest: Eat the covenant meal, the bread and the wine, those symbols by which you are a joint heir with Christ the Beloved.

Guest: And now, I, Jesus Christ, pray for you . . . that you have days of peace, joy and righteousness because Holy Spirit is in you and with you.

Guest: . . . that you have prosperity and health, for these are your inheritance . . .

Guest: . . . that your days are filled with purpose and meaning, accomplishments and anointing . . .

Guest: . . . always have heavenly days . . . even while you live on the earth.

Host: These things and so much more, I pray for you.

I am Jesus, and I love you.

Amen.

The Fourth Cup: The Cup of Praise

[The fourth cups are filled.]

Host: Let's stand and give praise and honor to our Lord Jesus Christ!

[Have a wonderful time of praise and worship.]

Host: Now we lift up the Cup of Praise to You—"That Someone" promised in the Garden long ago . . .

Guest: "That Someone" Who brought down the prideful status of the enemy . . .

Guest: "That Someone" Who reconciled us to God, making peace by His own blood . . .

Guest: "That Someone" Who has made us kings and priests to our God . . .

Guest: "That Someone" through Whom every family of the earth can be blessed!

Everyone: Lord Jesus, to You be the glory and honor, the majesty and power, forever and ever!

          You ARE "That Someone" Whom we love!

[Everyone drinks the fourth cup.]

Host: And now—

          May the promises of His blood covenant,

The power of His Word,

The presence of Holy Spirit, forever keep you—

Until Jesus comes again!

Amen.

PRAYER OF SALVATION

If you would like to know this wonderful Jesus as your Savior and Lord, please pray this prayer.

Dear Heavenly Father,

I believe that Jesus took all my sins when He died on the Cross.

I believe that He rose from the grave and now offers eternal life to me.

I repent of my sins and accept this offer of eternal life that Jesus purchased for me by His wounds and by His blood.

Please fill me with Your Holy Spirit.

Thank You that I am born again and part of the family of God.

In Jesus' Name,

Amen.

Endnotes

Entering the Blood Covenant

p. 8: "Strong friendship"
Trumbull, H.C. The Blood Covenant.
Impact Christian Books, Inc. Kirkwood. MO. 1975. p.18

pp. 9-11: The Steps of the blood covenant are adapted from:
Wolmarans, T. Blood Covenant. Word of Faith Publishing.
Dallas, TX. 1984. pp. 16-20; 24, 29-34, 39

p. 17
Strong, James. LL.D., S.T.D. The New Strong's Exhaustive
Concordance of the Bible. Thomas Nelson Publishers.
Nashville, TN. 1996. OT:7886

Scripture References

I. The People and the Blood Covenant

A.   Introduction
Genesis 1:24, 29
Genesis 3:1-21
Genesis 8:20, 21
Genesis 12:1-3
Exodus 12:1-3; 29:10-15
Psalm 2:7
Psalm 16:11
Psalm 20:2
Psalm 40:6-8
Isaiah 14:12-15
Ephesians 2:4
Hebrews 1:5
Hebrews 2:14-16
Hebrews 6:19; 10:5-9; 11:3
I Peter 1:12
I John 4:7

B.   Entering the Blood Covenant
Genesis 11:29, 30
Genesis 12
Genesis 14:18-20
Genesis 15
Genesis 17
Genesis 21:23-32
Genesis 22
Leviticus 7:2
Leviticus 17:11
I Samuel 18:4; 20:12-17
Psalm 2:7
Psalm 16:11

Psalm 40:6-8
Proverbs 18:24
Isaiah 41:8
II Corinthians 6:18
Galatians 3:13-29
Hebrews 10:5-24

C. Painting the Picture
Genesis 3:15; 49:10
Numbers 24:17
Psalm 45:7/Hebrews 1:9
Isaiah 9:2/Matthew 4:16
Ezekiel 1:26, 27
Matthew 9:35, 36
Luke 1:78
John 1:29, 32-34
Acts 10:38

II. That Someone

Genesis 3:15, 22:8
Leviticus 16
Exodus 12
Psalm 22:6
Matthews 26:1-5
Mark 11:1-11; 14:3-9
Luke 19:35-40
Luke 22
Luke 23:33
John 1:29; 12:9; 14:6; 17:5; 20:1-17
Ephesians 2:14, 15; 6:17
Hebrews 9:12
Hebrews 10:3, 4, 12, 20

III. The Bread and The Wine

A.   <u>Introduction</u>
Luke 22:14-16
John 1:29-36 (29, 36)
Revelation 5:6, 7, 13

B.   <u>The First Cup</u>
Exodus 2:23
Exodus 12
Exodus 13:3
Exodus 19:4
Exodus 30:19
John 13:1-5
Acts 2:1-4
Acts 4:29-31
Romans 8:2
Colossians 1:13
Ephesians 2:12, 18
I John 1:9
Revelation 1:5,6

C.   <u>The Second Cup</u>
Genesis 15:13, 17; 47:25
Exodus 1:8-22
Exodus 2:23-25
Exodus 5:10-19
Exodus 12
Psalm 6:3
Psalm 13:1
Psalm 91:10, 11
Ecclesiastes 3:11
Isaiah 43:19; 53:3-5; 55:8
John 19: 23, 33; 20:30, 21
Acts 2:2
I Corinthians 15:56

II Corinthians 5:7; 10:4
Colossians 1:14
Hebrews 5:9
I Peter 1:19; 2:24
I John 5:7

D.   The Third Cup
Genesis 3:6-14
Isaiah 53:3-12
Matthew 3:16, 17; 9:28-35
Mark 14:10, 11
Luke 7:1-14; 22:20
John 14:9; 17:24
I Corinthians 11:23-26
Galatians 3:13, 14
Hebrews 2:9-14
II Peter 1:3, 2:3
III John 2

1. Gethsemane
Genesis 3:1-5, 15
Exodus 12
Leviticus 16:20-22
Psalm 40:6-8
Matthew 3:16, 17
Mark 9:1-8
Luke 4:3, 13
Luke 22
John 8:29
John 9:4
Hebrews 2:14

2. The Crucifixion
Joshua 2:9-18
Psalm 22
Isaiah 53:12; 54:8

Matthew 27:28, 46, 51
Mark 15
Luke 23
John 19:26-30
Acts 1:15
II Corinthians 5:19-21
Revelation 1:6

3. The Burial of Jesus
   Matthew 27:57-60
   John 19:38-41

4. The Descent
   Genesis 3:15
   Deuteronomy 32:40,41
   Psalm 16
   Psalm 18:10-15
   Psalm 45:6, 7
   Isaiah 49:22; 50:8; 53:11; 59:16
   Ezekiel 1:16-21
   Acts 2:27, 31
   Colossians 1:15
   Ephesians 6:17
   Hebrews 1:9; 2:14; 12:24
   I John 3:8
   Revelation 1:18; 12:7-9

5. The Resurrection
   Genesis 3:15
   Genesis 12:1-3; 28:14
   Isaiah 53:5
   Matthew 27:33; 28:2
   Luke 23:40-43; 24:1-12
   John 20:11-17
   Hebrews 2:10-13; 7:16
   Revelation 22

6. The Ascension
   Leviticus 16:15
   Numbers 23:19
   Deuteronomy 11:21
   II Chronicles 5:11-14
   Ecclesiastes 3:11
   Isaiah 53:5
   Zechariah 12:10
   Luke 9:44; 22:15-20; 24:13-35
   John 1:14; 3:16-18; 14:13, 16-26; 16:13-15
   I Corinthians 10:4, 16
   Ephesians 6:10-18
   Hebrews 1:6-14; 6:13-18; 9:7, 11-28
   I John 5:7
   III John 2
   Revelation 12:11
   Revelation 19:16

E.   The Fourth Cup
   Genesis 28:14
   Colossians 1:13-15
   Ephesians 2:13-18
   Revelation 1:6
   Revelation 4:11

Bibliography

Bible History Online. "Bethany: Bible Cities—Bible History Links (Ancient Biblical Studies)." *Bible History Online*, 2010. Web. 14 Dec. 2010 <http://www.biblehistory.com/links.php?cat=40&sub=517&cat_name=Bible+Cities&subcat_name=Bethany>.

_____. "Fig Trees: Manners & Customs—Bible History Links (Ancient Biblical Studies)." *Bible History Online*, 2010. Web. 14 Dec. 2010 <http://www.biblehistory.com/links.php?cat=39&sub=720&cat_name=Manners+%26+Customs&subcat_name=Fig+Trees>.

Edersheim, Alfred. The Life and Times of Jesus the Messiah: New Updated Edition. USA. Hendrickson Publishers, Inc. 1993. Print.

Latner, Helen. *The Book of Modern Jewish Etiquette*. New York: Schocken Books, 1981. Print.

Passover Haggadah. KF Holdings, Inc., 2003.

Shepherd, Coulson. *Jewish Holy Days: Their Prophetic and Christian Significance.* Neptune, NJ: Loizeaux Brothers, Inc., 1961. Print.

Strong, James. "Shiloh." *The New Strong's Exhaustive Concordance of the Bible.* Nashville: Thomas Nelson, Inc., 1995. Print.

Trumbull, H. Clay. *The Blood Covenant.* Kirkwood, MO: Impact Christian Books, Inc., 1975. Print.

Wolmarans, Theo. *Blood Covenant.* Dallas: Word of Faith Publishing, 1984. Print.

Host's Guidelines

INTRODUCTION

To host "That Someone" is to invite The Lord Jesus into your presence. Memorable moments await those who join in this time of fellowship, praise and worship, fun, laughter, and joy. Please walk through this journey with us and with "That Someone."

BIBLICAL FOUNDATIONS

The purpose of this work is to give the followers of Jesus a deeper personal insight into the love of the Father, The Son, and The Holy Spirit. This love, expressed in the holiness of the blood covenant instituted by Them, gave birth to a Redeemer Who has reconciled all of creation back to God. The footprints of the blood covenant can be found throughout the Scriptures. In this work, the foundational scriptures are:

- Genesis 1:26-28
- Genesis 3
- Genesis 12-22
- Exodus 1-14
- Matthew 26-28
- Mark 14-16
- Luke 22-24
- I Corinthians 11:20-31
- Galatians 3:13-29
- Hebrews 1-13

These scriptures, as well as others, woven throughout the script provide a solid foundational framework. Another component exists, however, which is of utmost importance in creating the atmosphere where The Father, The Son, and The Holy Spirit are free to move. When we go through the ceremony of taking communion, or of eating the elements of the Passover which foreshadow Christ the Passover Lamb (I Cor. 5:7), we want this to be done in the sense of an "open communion." By this we mean that this participation is open to all who have confessed Jesus Christ as Lord and Savior.

If you, as the host, want to use this time as an evangelical opportunity to share the love of Jesus and the power of the blood covenant, then the born-again leader/host should do the ceremony as a demonstration, using the elements to explain the mysteries of God. In this setting, he or she alone would eat and drink the Passover and Communion foods. The Afikomen, which is the "hidden bread of life" can still be hidden and searched for, but would not be distributed among the group. When found, it would be returned to the leader. This fulfills the boundaries set in Exodus 12:43-48(that those who ate the Passover were in blood covenant agreement with the Lord God), and in I Corinthians 11:26-29, (that those who take Communion are in blood covenant agreement with the Lord Jesus Christ, and that they partake in a manner that honors that status).

PREPARATIONS

My family and I hosted this celebration for over a decade. During that time, we grew (some times through trial and error) in our understanding of the preparation that was needed. Listed below are some of the foundational activities that have brought success.

Prayer

Prayer and intercession provide the groundwork for any successful endeavor, and this one is no exception. Many times during the weeks before the celebration I found myself drawn to an increased time of prayer and repentance. I Corinthians 5:7, 8, in speaking of Christ as our Passover Lamb, tells us to purge out the old leaven of the flesh.

By His grace and mercy, by His complete and perfect redemption, we become new creatures in Christ. We become "the unleavened bread of sincerity and truth."

Therefore, as the leader and host, spend some time in prayer. Pray for yourself and for others to come and experience being in the presence of the Lord. After all, you *are* hosting the One Who is "That Someone" Who made it easy to find our Father in Heaven once again.

Dates and Times

While this celebration is designed to coincide with the Easter and Passover season, separate components are also ideal for individual or small group use. The Third and Fourth Cup in "The Bread and The Wine" section are ideally suited for a Communion setting. Our meetings were always held on Good Friday evening for several reasons; the main one being that the subject matter concerns the Passover and the Last Passover Supper of Jesus Christ. Other considerations were that many of our friends were free on that evening and did not have to work the next day. The full ceremony can take two hours. We usually had dinner and fellowship prior to this, so that a full evening was required. Having said this, I must add that this time became, over the years, one that we looked forward to with great expectancy and joy!

Props

The physical props may be as simple or elaborate as you like. Those that are of primary importance include the recognition that you are "hosting" the presence of "That Someone", Jesus Christ. This will require a chair in His honor and a small table set with a small plate and goblet (or cup) to symbolize the blood covenant meal. The plate and cup should be covered with a beautiful napkin to symbolize the glory that overshadows the holy blood of the covenant of God.

Please remember to point out this "seating" as you begin the celebration. This will help to remind everyone that He is with us, celebrating, singing, laughing and joining in the joy of His people gathering together.

Two sets of role-playing occur during the Blood Covenant section. An explanation is given before these begin stating that, in this dispensation, the blood of our Lord Jesus Christ that was shed at Calvary is the only blood that has power in Heaven and on earth.

Therefore, during this role-play, no blood of any kind is ever to be shed. The purpose of these interactions is to illustrate the framework that God the Father used to paint the portrait of His Son as the Redeemer. Having said this, here are some of the props needed for the "Adams and Bailey" scene:
- some carpenter tools/paint brushes
- a package wrapped in brown paper to resemble fish
- a large key (for the open air stall)
- two car keys (for the Ferraris)
- a navy blue business blazer
- a fleece jacket

Format

The format is informal; a time of inviting family and friends together to celebrate the "great salvation" that our Lord Jesus Christ has purchased for us. We start with dinner and fellowship, which provides time to share and renew friendships. As host, one of the main concerns will be to transition in a smooth and timely fashion to the celebration format.

There are two main sections: "The Blood Covenant" and "The Bread and The Wine" (Seder). We strongly encourage having two hosts, one for each section. We believe this provides the greatest ease and enjoyment for everyone.

As with any social event, the number of people to invite will vary. Over the years we have had attendance range from as little as seven to as many as thirty. The most comfortable group seems to be between twelve and twenty. Please remember that children are a welcome addition to any group. This celebration truly desires to pass on the story of the greatness of our God to the next generation!

Food Preparations

The food supply for the celebration primarily includes the elements that are found in a Passover Seder. Remember to ask your guest about any food allergies. One year some of our guests had nut allergies, so we made special dishes for them.

Foods for "The Bread and The Wine" section include:

- Grape juice: [enough for four small cups/person]
- A box of matzah
- A bunch of parsley
- A mixture of salt water [you can make this yourself]
- Horseradish [the bitter herbs]
- Charoset [a mixture of chopped apples, grape juice, crushed walnuts, cinnamon; commercial mixtures are also available]
- Water
- Small cups, plates, and napkins

The leader/host's plate and table should include:

- A sectioned plate/(Seder) plate that consists of the following:

  Parsley
  A small cup of salt water
  Horseradish
  Charoset
  A lamb bone

  A roasted or boiled egg

- Five cups/goblets for juice (The Cup of Elijah plus the four cups of the meal)
- A bread plate with three matzahs, each separated by a napkin and covered on top by a final napkin. [During the ceremony, the middle matzah or Afikomen, will be broken in half. One half is returned to its place between the napkins; the other half is hidden and later searched out.]
- Three Shabbat candles ["The Lighting of the Candles" section]
- A small bowl of water and a towel ["The Washing of the Hands" section] A box of wet towelettes is needed for the group hand washing in " The Bread and The Wine" section, The First Cup.

Music

What is a celebration without music? We begin our celebrations with a time of prayer and singing. Choose the music that you love and create an atmosphere that brings joy to The Father, The Son, and The Spirit. You may also include songs between the "cup" segments in "The Bread and The Wine" section.

Conclusion

May this experience bring you the love of Heaven, the peace of God, the fellowship of the Holy Spirit.

May "That Someone" bring blessings to your life and be the fulfillment of Genesis 28:14 and Galatians 3:16, 17, that is, through Jesus Christ all the families of the earth have the opportunity to be blessed.

In His love,

Chiquita Hayes, M.D.